All Around the Pond

Written and Illustrated by
Joni Prew

Joni Prew
Circle Time Productions

Joni Prew
Circle Time Productions

All rights reserved.

No parts of this book may be reproduced, stored in a retrieval system, or transmitted in any form, by any means, including mechanical, electronic, photocopying, recording or otherwise without the prior consent of the author or publisher.

Published by Circle Time Productions
printed by KDP/Amazon
Words © 2022
Revised illustrations © 2024
ISBN: 9798751543556
BISAC: JNF003340/JNF003090/JNF003250

A pond is a still body of fresh water that is surrounded by land.

Dedicated to Ali –
the one who helped me to appreciate the little things.

All around the pond

lounging on a lily pad

I spy a frog

life really isn't too bad

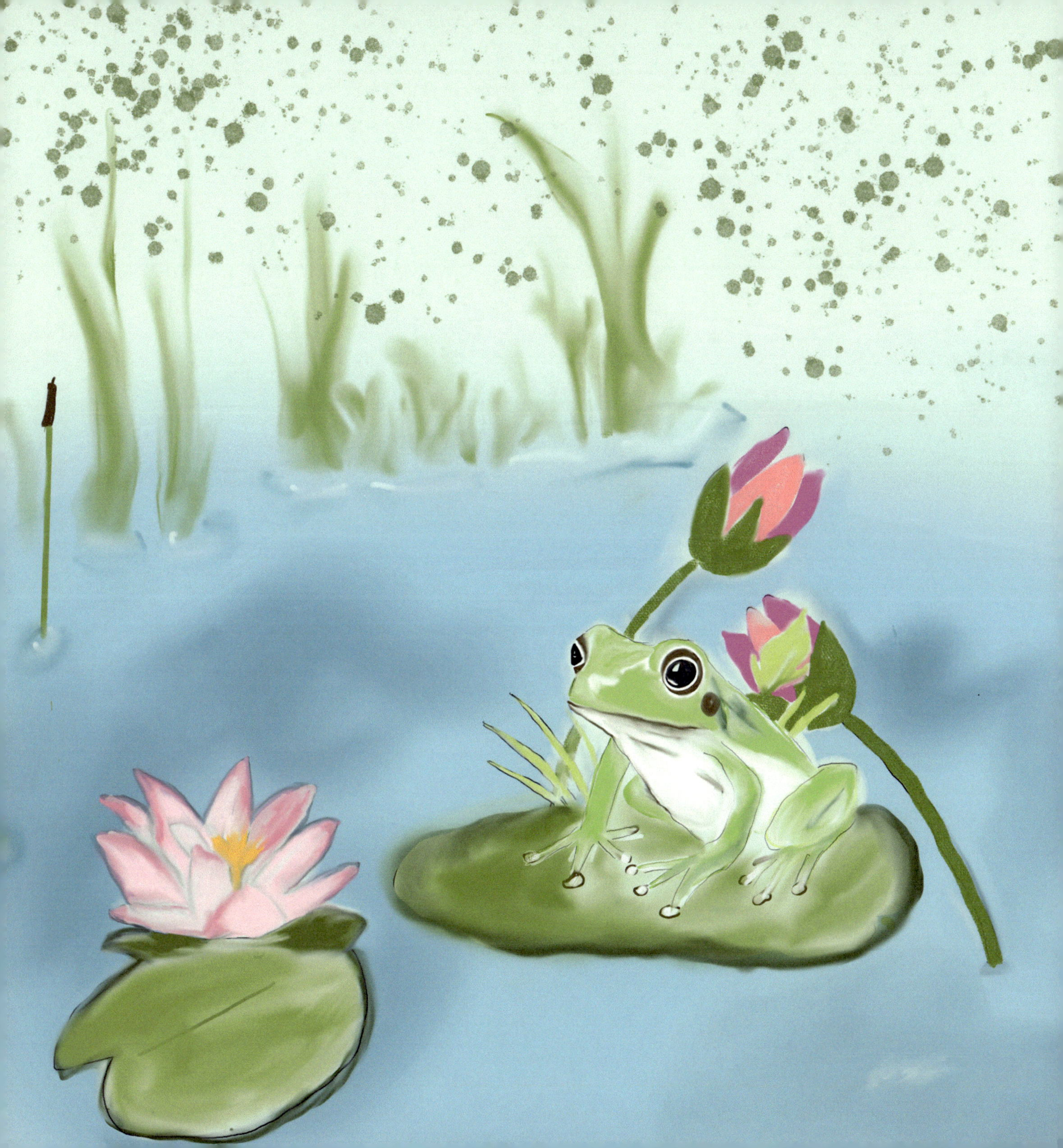

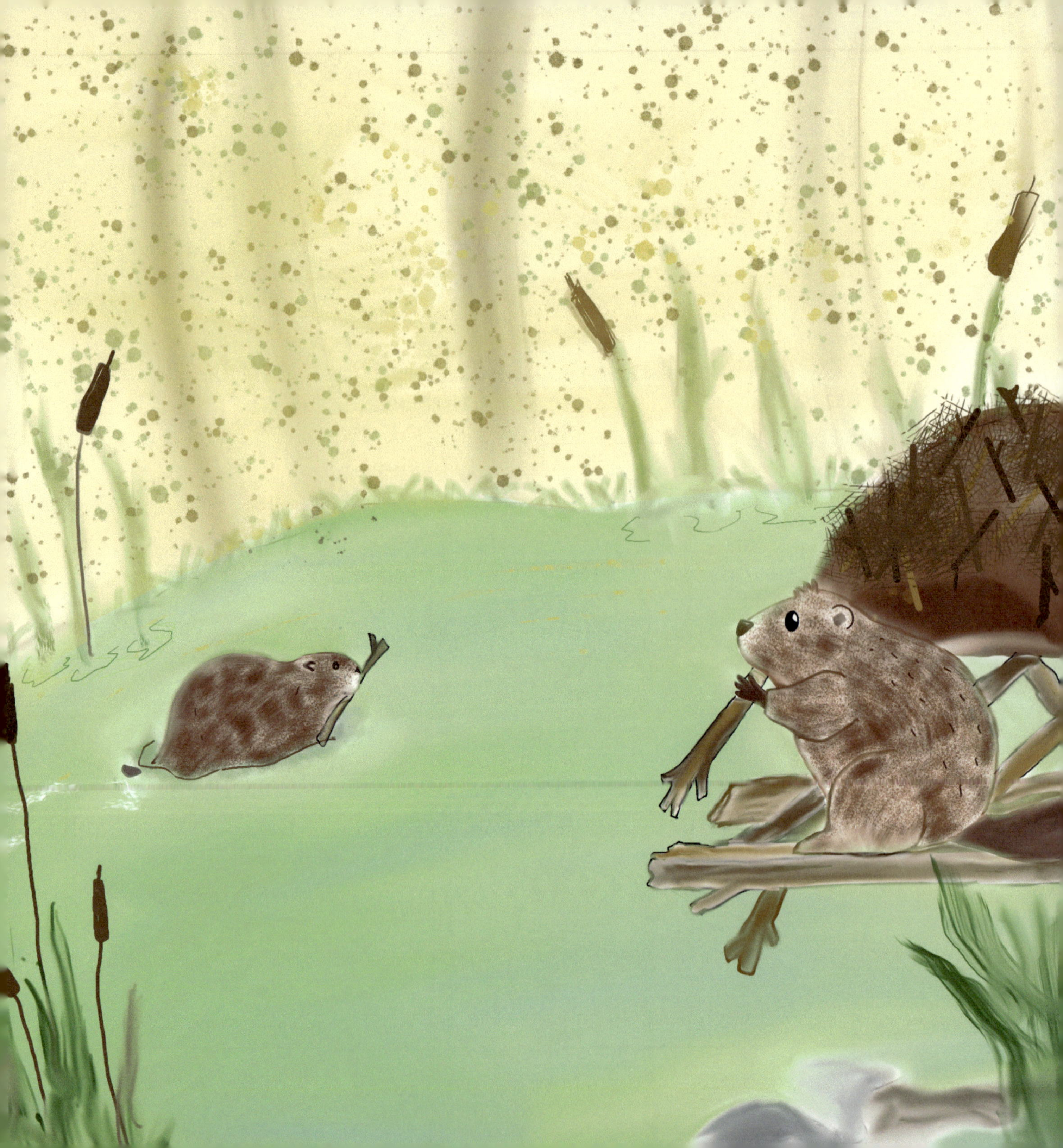

All around the pond cutting down some trees I spy a beaver damming up the water - oh geez!

All around the pond

swimming with his friends

I spy a fish

sparkling as it bends

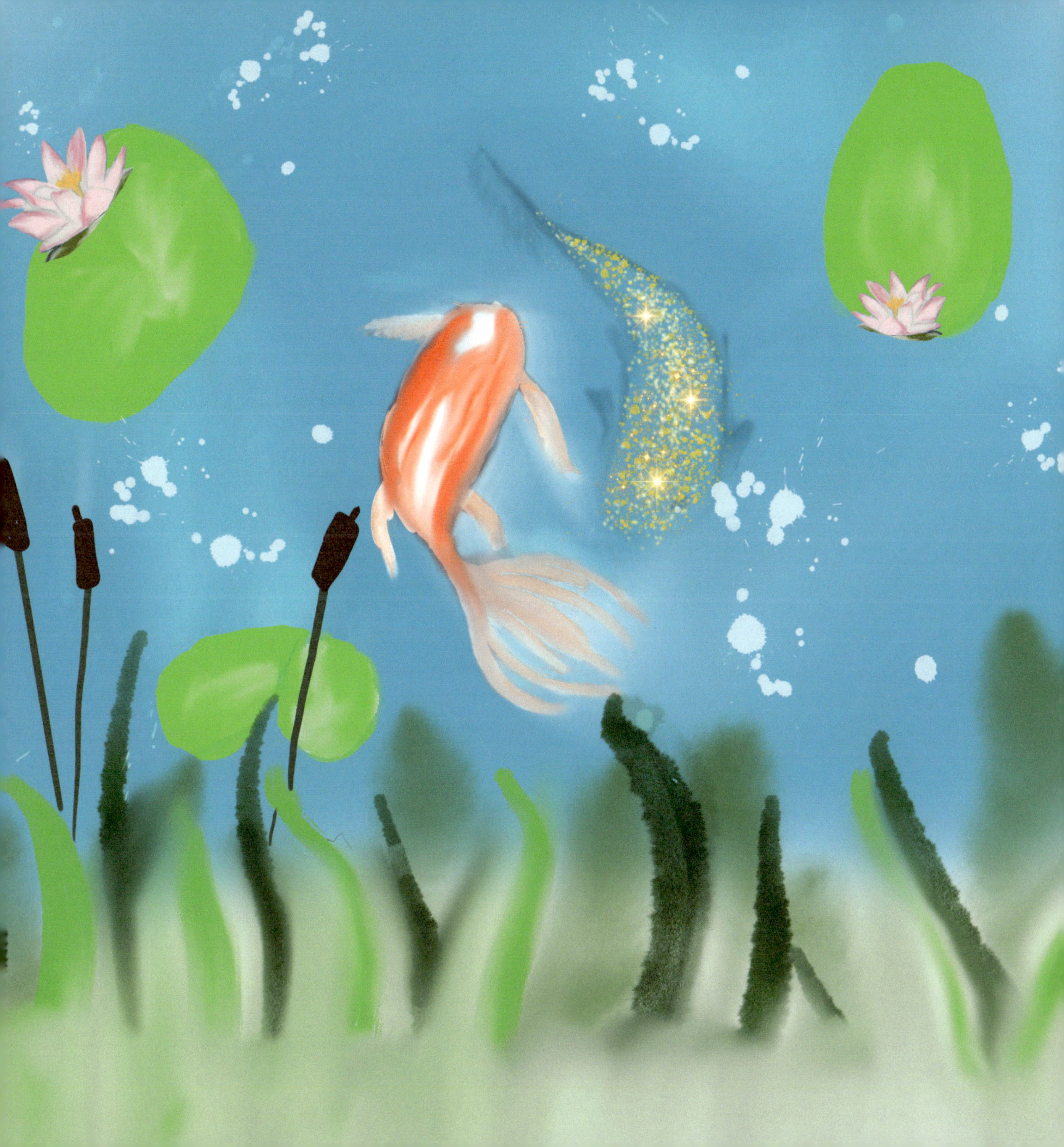

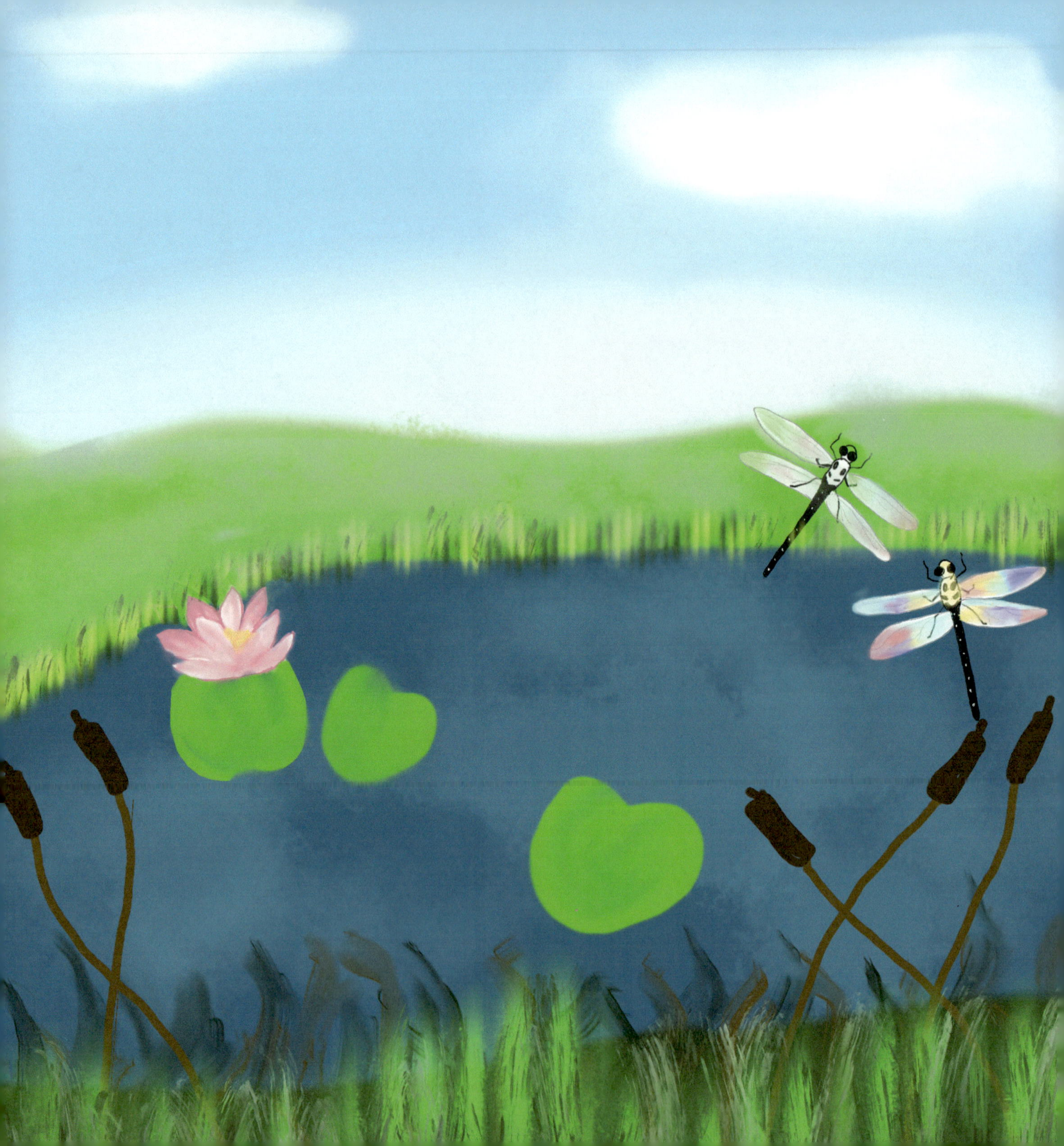

All around the pond
darting through the air
I spy a dragonfly
Oh look! - there's a pair!

All around the pond

paddling to and fro

I spy a duck

I wonder where she'll go

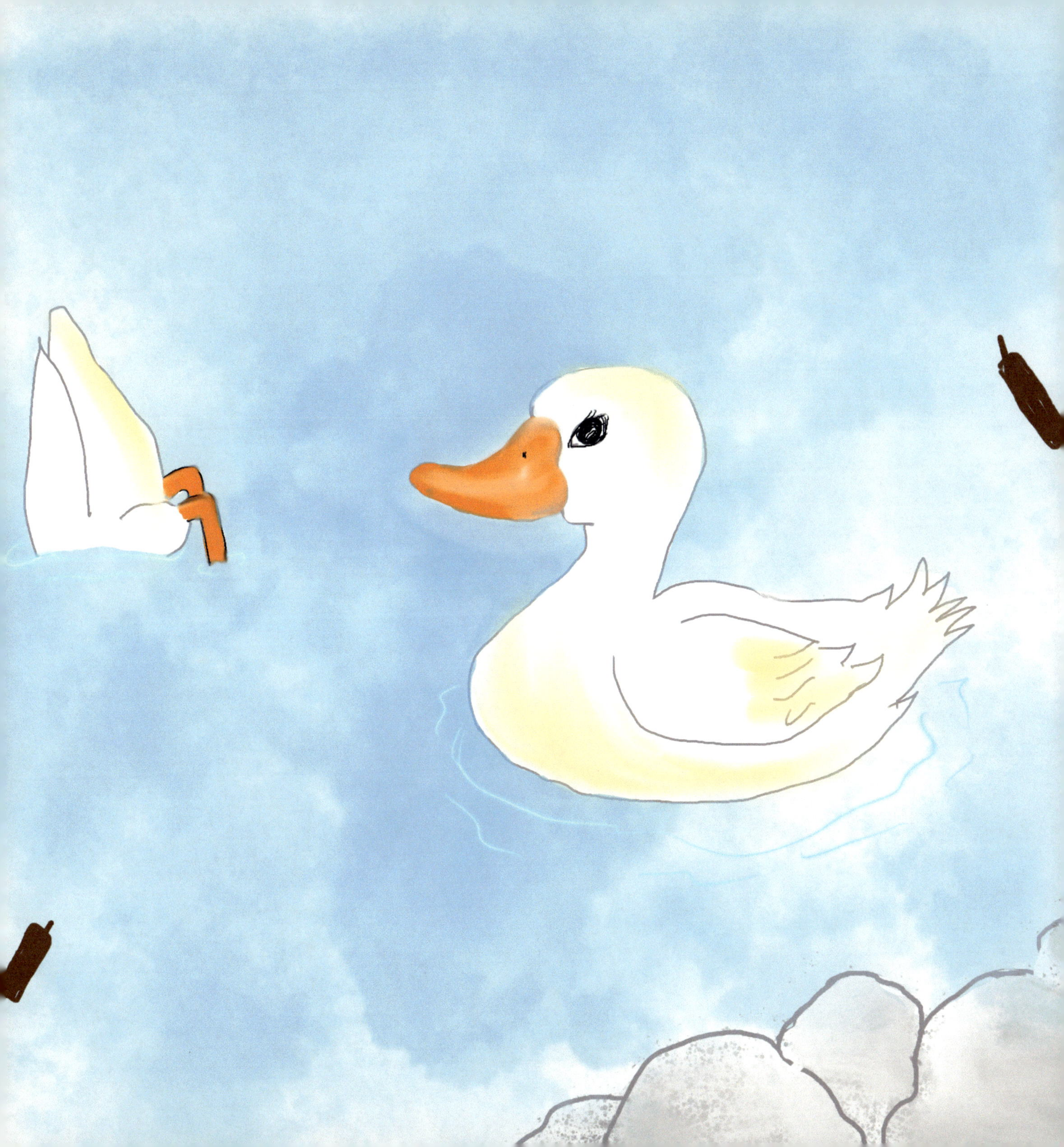

Go Away!

All around the pond
buzzing in the air
I spy some mosquitoes
I think they're in my hair!

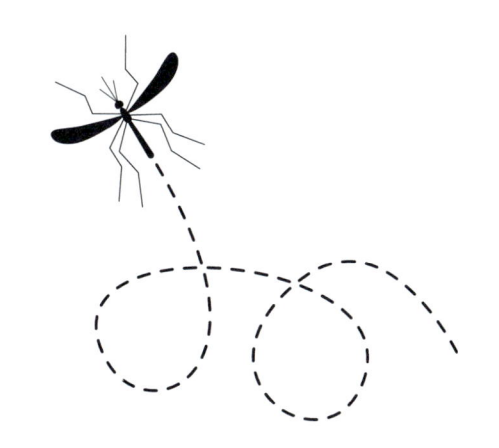

All around the pond
sliding down the slimy slope
I spy a snapping turtle
Friendly? I say, "Nope".

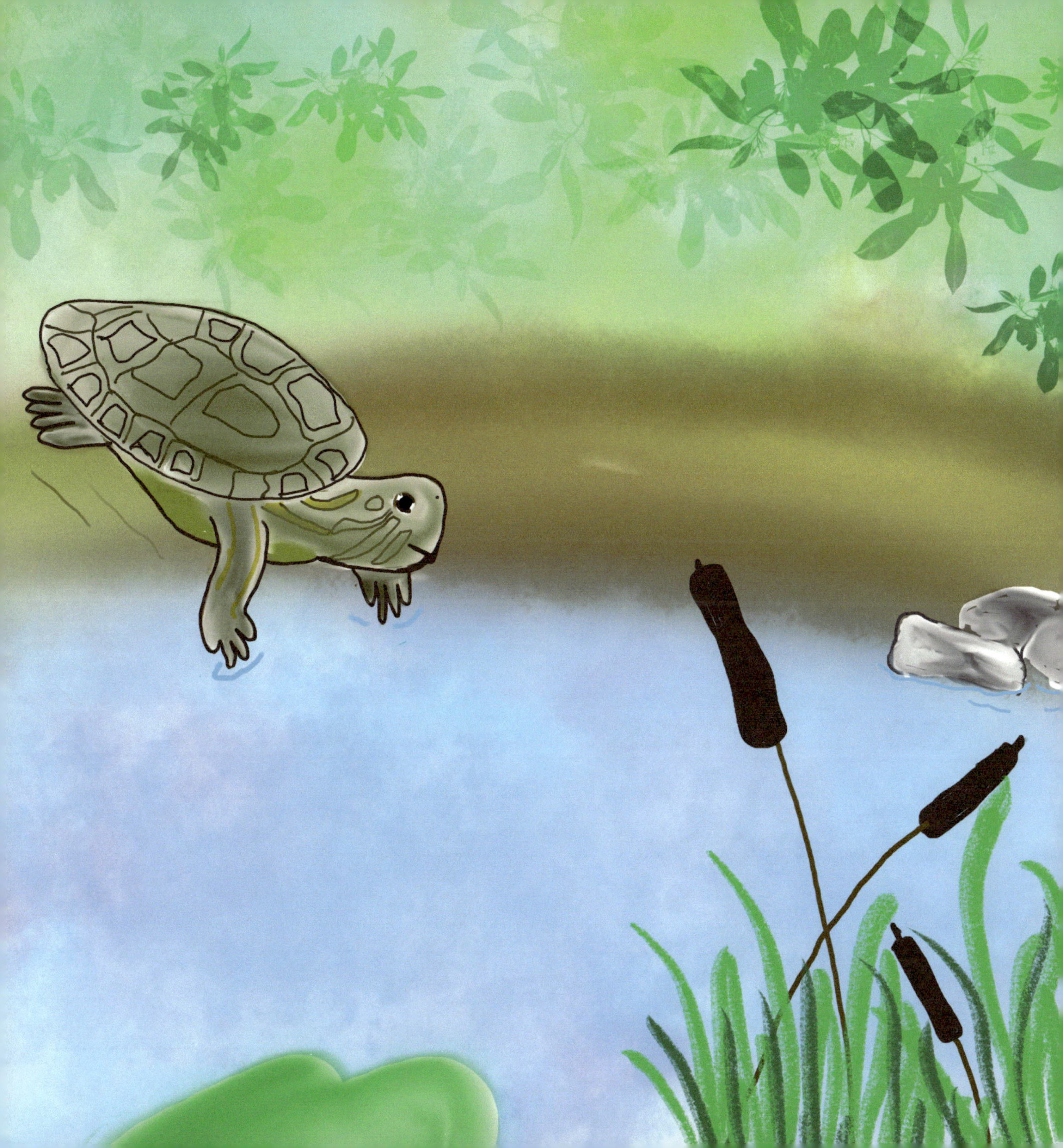

All around the pond
All around
You will find...
Big animals,
Small animals,
So many kinds...

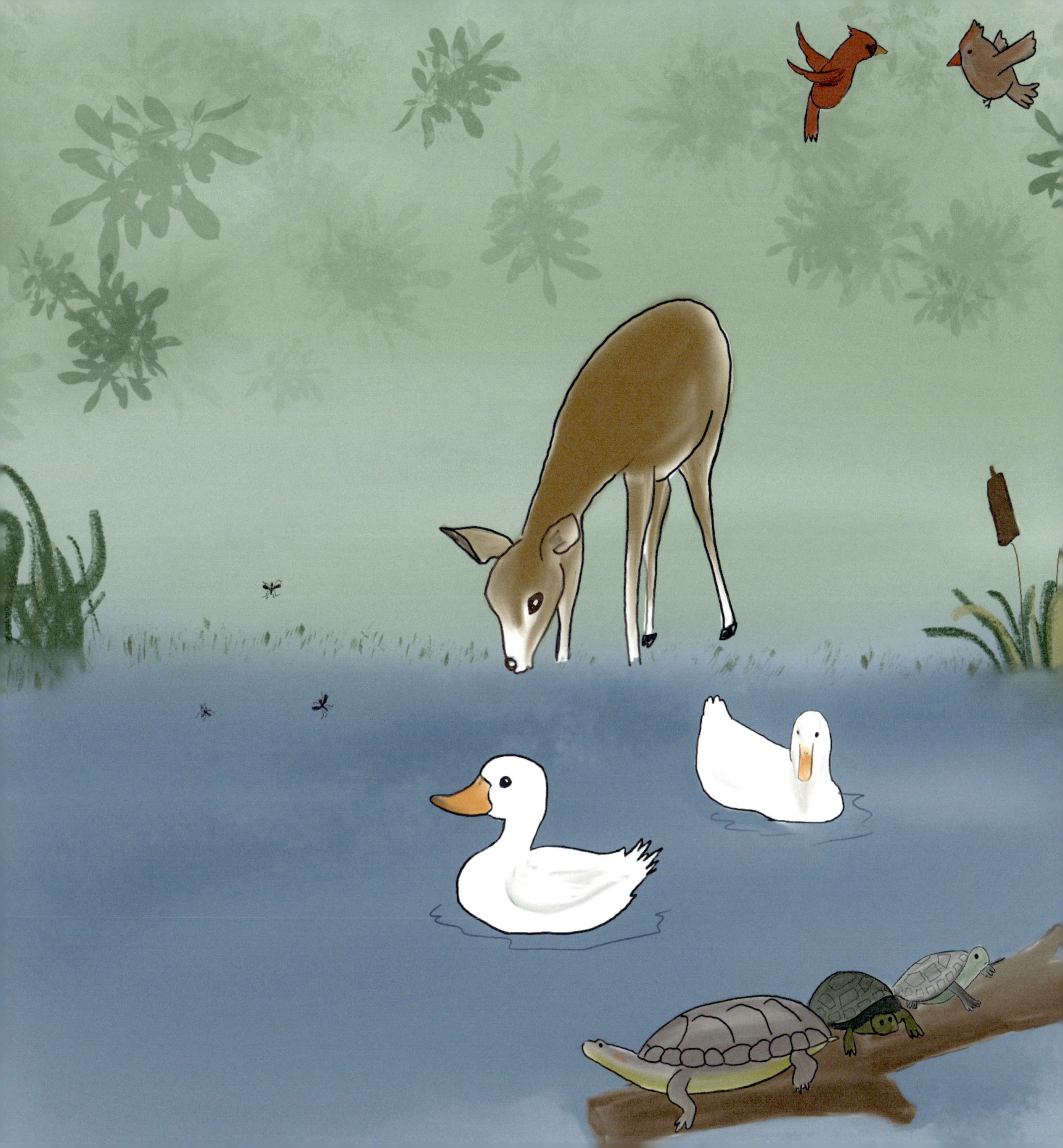

The End

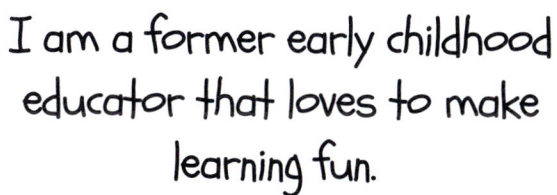

Joni Prew
Circle Time Productions

Other books in the "Animals in Natural Habitats" series

Into the Jungle
Under the Ocean
Throughout the Forest
Across the Desert
At the North and South Poles

I am a former early childhood educator that loves to make learning fun.
I was born in Connecticut, I graduated with a Masters in Early Childhood Education and taught elementary school children for almost 20 years. I am married to my amazing husband, Terry, and we have one daughter, Ali. I have the sweetest dog (Marley) and two crazy cats (Salem and Teddy).
I currently live in North Carolina. When not writing or illustrating books, I enjoy golfing, gardening, hiking and crafting.

Other books by Joni Prew:

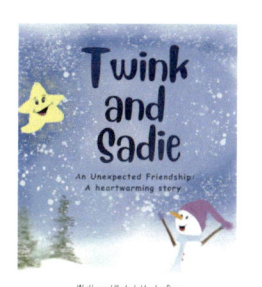

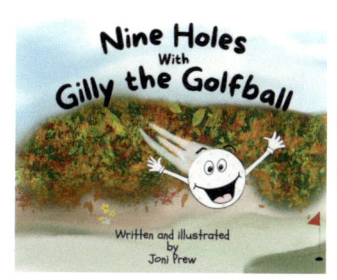

Twink and Sadie
An Unexpected Friendship: A heartwarming story
Written and Illustrated by Joni Prew

Nine Holes With Gilly the Golfball
Written and illustrated by Joni Prew

The "Animals in Natural Habitat" series provides lots of learning opportunities in science, language & reading.

Visit our website for fun activities to do with each of our books. Sign up for the CTP newsletter to get any new updates.
(I hate spam so, we promise not to spam you!)

Joni Prew
Circle Time Productions

www.circletimeproductions.com

The best compliment you can give an author or illustrator is to leave a review for their book and recommend it to others.

If you liked this book, you can leave a review on Amazon, OakieBees.com or our website www.circletimeproductions.com

Made in the USA
Columbia, SC
30 October 2024